GYMNASTICS

JACQUIE LEAVY

Wayland

Go For Sport
Basketball
Cricket
Fishing
Gymnastics
Judo
Karate
Rugby
Soccer

Safety note: Many of the moves in this book should only be performed by experienced gymnasts with the aid of a coach. Do not attempt to perform any of the moves outside a gym or without the supervision of a gymnastics instructor.

Cover: Betty Okino of the USA in the 1992 world championships.

Picture acknowledgements
The publisher would like to thank Eileen Langsley/Supersport Photographs for providing all of the pictures used in this book.

The author would like to thank the following for their help in compiling this book: Mitch Fenner, Mike Swallow and the Hillingdon School Of Gymnastics, Sarah Van Hesteren and Marion Sands.

Series Editor: James Kerr
Book Editor: Alison Field
Designer: Malcolm Walker

First published in 1993 by
Wayland (Publishers) Limited,
61 Western Road,
Hove, East Sussex, BN3 1JD

© Copyright 1993 Wayland (Publishers) Limited

British Library Cataloguing in Publication Data
Leavy, Jacqueline
   Gymnastics. - (Go for Sport! Series)
   I. Title II. Series
   796.44

ISBN 0-7502-0664-0

Typeset by Kudos Editorial and Design Services
Printed and bound in Italy by G.Canale and C.S.p.A.

Contents

INTRODUCTION

Gymnastics has a long and colourful heritage. The Greeks originally developed the sport in the eighth century BC, and to them it was as important as art and music. They discovered that gymnastics could change the shape and strength of the human body.

The Germans revived interest in gymnastics in the nineteenth century when Friedrich Jahn opened an outdoor gymnasium near Berlin in 1811. Jahn was the first person to use the parallel bars and horizontal bar, and he sent teams of gymnasts on tour. Jahn's gymnastics concentrated on muscular development. His contemporary, Henrich Ling, the Swedish father of gymnastics, concentrated on freedom of movement and free expression. Both branches of gymnastics are incorporated in today's sport.

The Olympic Games

Gymnastics was included in the first modern Olympic Games in Athens in 1896, and the competition was dominated by the Germans. Women did not compete until 1928, when a team competition was held. After the first men's world championships in Basle in 1950, which the Swiss won, men's gymnastics was dominated by the Soviet Union.

The first star of the women's competition was Larissa Latynina. In three Olympics she won nine gold, five silver and three bronze medals, and was the individual overall champion twice. Just as gymnastics was gaining an international audience through TV, the Mexico Games in 1968 produced the biggest star of gymnastics yet, Vera Caslavska from Czechoslovakia, who won four gold medals. Caslavska was succeeded by the USSR's Ludmilla Tourischeva as the queen of the gymnastics arena.

However, the undisputed star of the Munich Olympics in 1972 was Tourischeva's team-mate, Olga Korbut. With her impish charm, this tiny slip of a girl (1.50 m in height and just 38 kg in weight) put gymnastics well and truly on the map. Although she could only manage golds on the beam and floor and a silver on bars, finishing just seventh overall, Korbut was the name on everyone's lips at these Games. Such was the storm caused by the 'Munchkin of Munich' that when Japan's Kato became only the third man in history to take the men's overall title twice, it was hardly given a second thought.

Four years down the line, another tiny gymnast hijacked the Olympic headlines. Nadia Comaneci, a fourteen-year-old Romanian girl, exploded on to the gymnastics scene. Scoring the first ever perfect 10, for her asymmetric bars exercise, Comaneci heralded a new era in women's gymnastics. She went on to score six more 10s in the course of the competition, taking the overall Olympic title ahead of the Soviet star, Nelli Kim. At the Moscow Games in 1980, Comaneci narrowly failed in her defence of the title, losing to Elena Davydova (USSR) by just 0.075 of a mark.

The 1984 Los Angeles Games were affected by boycott. The Soviet Union team, amongst others, stayed

Olga Korbut, the 'Munchkin of Munich', won the hearts of the crowd with her cheeky choreography for the floor exercise during the 1972 Olympic Games.

Nadia Comaneci stole the headlines and the medals, and made gymnastics history, by scoring the first ever 10 - the maximum number of marks - for her asymmetric bars routine during the Montreal Olympic Games in 1976.

gold medal. Her coach was equally delighted, as she was his second overall champion in three Olympics. Bela Karolyi, having guided Comaneci to gold in 1976, defected to the USA to bring his coaching genius to the American squad.

The Seoul Olympics in 1988 saw all of the leading gymnastics nations competing again in the Olympics for the first time since 1976. In the women's event there was a tremendous battle between Romania's Daniela Silivas and the USSR's Yelena Shushunova for the overall title. It was the last event, the vault, that decided the gold medal-list. The winner was Shushunova by 0.05 of a mark. In the men's section the Soviet team were dominant, taking all three medals in the overall event, and the team title.

For once, in the 1992 Olympic competition, it was the men who stole the show. Vitaly Scherbo of the CIS team (formerly the Soviet Union team) won six gold medals; more than any other athlete at the Olympic Games, and a gymnastics record. He took the overall gold and team gold plus the pommel, rings, vault and parallel bars individual titles. In the women's

away. Everyone expected the Romanians to march off with all the medals. Ecatarina Szabo was the new star of the Romanian camp – a daredevil gymnast, who was a natural tumbler and had a bubbly personality. But in the Pauley Pavilion in Los Angeles she couldn't out-smile or out-perform the eventual overall winner. To the delight of the home crowd, Mary Lou Retton clinched the

competition the world champion, Kim Zmeskal, of whom much was expected, fell from the beam with virtually her first step of the competition. She never really recovered her true form, and finished just tenth overall. The major battle for gold was between two gymnasts who were as alike as twins. The USA's Shannon Miller and Tatiana Gutsu of the CIS were neck-and-neck in a titanic battle for gold, despite Gutsu's fall from the beam early on in the competition. However, Gutsu just got better and better, and pipped Miller for the gold.

Other types of gymnastics

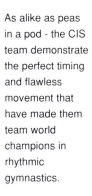

As alike as peas in a pod - the CIS team demonstrate the perfect timing and flawless movement that have made them team world champions in rhythmic gymnastics.

A second branch of gymnastics was introduced into the Games in 1984 – rhythmic gymnastics. This is an all-women sport that arrived in Britain in its earliest form about 100 years ago. It evolved from the Swedish system of gymnastics in the nineteenth century. A Swiss teacher, Jacques Dalcroze, trained teachers in eurhythmics, which concentrated on free movement to music. Another early gymnast, Heinrich Medau, interlinked the music, dance and movement with apparatus work – with hoops, ball and clubs.

However, it was the Eastern Europeans who took rhythmic gymnastics by the scruff of the neck and developed it into the sport that exists today. The Fédération Internationale de Gymnastique (FIG) gave the new sport official recognition in 1962; the first world championships took place a year later and have been held every two years since.

The third and final branch of the sport is sports acrobatics. This concentrates on acrobatic feats and tumbling, and is spectacular to watch. It was developed in the Soviet Union and Eastern Europe, with the first ever sports acrobatics tournament being held in 1957 in Warsaw. Western countries gradually began to compete in this sport, which involves tumbling and gymnastic work in pairs, trios and fours. The Federation of Sports Acrobatics was formed in 1973, although the sport is not yet an Olympic one.

What does it take?

Gymnastics is one of the most demanding sports in existence. It places physical demands on the whole body and requires a gruelling training schedule and practice, practice, practice to become world class. If it is your chosen sport you can expect bruises, sweat and tears along the way. So why on earth do people do it? Well, no other sport presents quite such an all-round challenge. It requires control, precision, speed, strength, grace, agility, concentration, wits, courage, personality, determination and, above all else, discipline. There is nothing like mastering a new movement that just a few months before seemed an impossible dream; or performing that first back somersault, unaided, or that first free-cartwheel; or that feeling of achievement and satisfaction that comes from performing in competition to the best of your ability and maybe coming home with a medal.

Good gymnasts are supple and slim and have good extension and balance, grace and poise, good spring, and leg and arm strength. Several of these things can be learned through training. What cannot be learned is discipline and dedication to the sport. Only the truly dedicated make it to the very top in gymnastics, because it is such a demanding sport. If you want to be a really good gymnast, you have to be organized and disciplined, not only in the gym but in all areas of your life. It will mean coming home from school, doing all your homework and then going out to the gym to train (or vice versa). It may mean saying no to cakes and sweets, and missing out on the school disco because you've got a competition next day.

Despite the sacrifices, the rewards are immense and, even if you don't want to be the next Comaneci, gymnastics is a sport that is a lot of fun and one that will help you to make many lifelong friends.

One of the most elegant gymnasts, Svetlana Boguinskaia, shows superb extension in this handstand.

THE BASICS

What to wear

Female gymnasts wear leotards, usually made of a lycra fabric that allows maximum freedom of movement. When competing, artistic gymnasts usually stick to one leotard for the whole competition, because they often have to wear a number on their back. In rhythmic gymnastics however, gymnasts often change their leotards to create a different mood for each piece of apparatus, although this is not compulsory. There are several things to remember when you are dressing for the gym:

✪ Make sure that your leotard looks neat and tidy for competition. A sloppy appearance can affect your overall presentation.

✪ Tie up long hair out of the way, for reasons of safety and presentation.

✪ Gym shoes may be worn, and in rhythmic gymnastics the competitors often wear a half shoe that just covers the toes. However, for the best grip in any branch of the sport, bare feet are best.

✪ Remove all jewellery.

Male gymnasts wear shorts and a sleeveless leotard for the floor exercise and vault. For the other

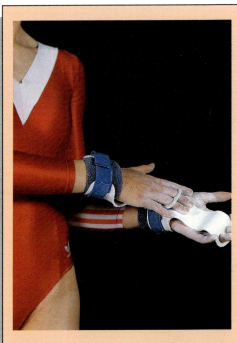

✪ *Tracksuits are worn by all gymnasts. Essential pieces of clothing, they are worn during warm-up and prevent the muscles getting cold between exercises at competitions.*

✪ *For artistic gymnastics, leather handguards are important, as they protect the hands and improve grip on the bars.*

✪ *Chalk or magnesium carbonate is sprinkled on the hands and apparatus by gymnasts. It keeps the hands dry and prevents friction burns.*

Daniela Silivas demonstrates poise, balance and extension on the beam.

pieces long, white, stretchy trousers are worn. Most male gymnasts opt to wear soft gym shoes, although this isn't compulsory.

Equipment

✪ **Artistic gymnastics:** In women's artistic gymnastics there are four pieces of apparatus: the vault, asymmetric bars, beam and floor. In the men's event there are six pieces of apparatus: the floor, parallel bars, pommel horse, high bar, rings and vault.

✪ **Rhythmic gymnastics:** In the rhythmic branch of the sport there are five pieces of hand apparatus: the rope, hoop, ball, clubs and ribbon. The apparatus are used by individual gymnasts and for group work.

✪ **Sports acrobatics:** The exercises in sports acrobatics are as follows: tumbling; women's pairs, men's pairs and mixed pairs; women's trios; men's fours.

Warming up

The warm-up is the most important part of your gym session. It is very tempting to go into the gymnasium and head straight for the apparatus – do not be tempted! Skipping warm-up is a sure way to suffer injuries such as pulled muscles or ligaments or even broken bones.

After you have been sitting in one place all day, such as the classroom, a good warm-up gets the blood circulating more quickly round the body, and this gives you more energy. It makes your joints more flexible and gives you better extension, so you are able to reach further.

By warming up you are preparing your body for the training session or competition ahead. After all, in gymnastics you are asking your body to bend and stretch in all sorts of ways it would not naturally do, so it is only fair to give it some warning! By taking time to do this preparation, you will find that moves are easier to perform, and you will be more alert in the gym.

Some coaches lead a warm-up for all members of the gym class to follow. If there is no set warm-up in your class, you can make up your own. Start with a short jog (for a few minutes) and then gently stretch out the parts of the body: the feet, ankles, legs, hips, back, shoulders, arms, wrists, hands and neck.

Try to keep the movements smooth; for example, rotate the hips in a big circle to stretch out the back, gradually making the circle bigger so that you are stretching further to the back each time. To warm up the legs, stand in front of a wall or wall bars, holding the bar or leaning on the wall. Then gently swing the leg up at the back, keeping your supporting leg straight.

The USA's Bart Conner prepares for competition with a thorough warm-up.

Once you are feeling supple, you can take your warm-up a bit further and go on to practise movements such as split jumps and walkovers. These two elements are good for stretching out the back and legs.

If you know that one part of your body is not particularly flexible, take a bit of extra time at the end of your warm-up to work on this. For example, if you don't have very supple legs, practise trying to get down into splits and holding the splits position. But take things gradually, especially if you can't quite manage the splits yet.

If you are unsure how to go about warming up a particular part of the body, your coach will be able to advise you of some exercises to do.

Dance

Dance, particularly ballet, has an enormous role to play in gymnastics, especially when it comes to choreographing a floor exercise. Many gymnastic movements, such as split jumps, pirouettes, arabesques and flexions, are taken from ballet. Dancers are renowned for their poise, grace and strength. For these reasons most coaches insist that their gymnasts attend some sort of ballet class. Repetition of ballet exercises improves a gymnast's leg strength and footwork.

A particularly good exercise that helps to build up leg strength and control is the developé. Start with the feet in first position (heels together and feet facing outwards, legs straight and knees together), holding on to a chair or a bar. Draw the outside leg up to the knee as if you are drawing a line from your ankle to your knee

The developé
Remember to keep the supporting leg strong and the body straight. Try not to lean or wobble in this movement.

with your toe. Slowly unfold the leg straight out in front of you with the knee facing the ceiling, and hold this position. This may make your muscles ache at first until you get used to doing it. This exercise is then repeated with the leg to the side and then to the back. Remember always to keep the supporting leg straight, and to hold the bar or chair only lightly – do not lean on it for support.

You and your coach

To progress in gymnastics you need to develop a good working relationship with your coach. You need to be able to listen to advice from your coach and then apply it to the movements you are doing in order to make the performance better, correct faults and iron out bad technique. Your coach is the most important person in your gymnastics career, so listen to what he or she has to say.

Learning new movements

When you tackle new moves you won't be able to do them first time. It's a good idea to break new moves down into smaller parts or skills. This may seem boring at the time, but the process of breaking movements down is how even the world's best gymnasts learn new skills.

✪　For example, if you are learning a free cartwheel you will start off learning just a cartwheel.

✪　You then progress to a cartwheel with a run-up.

✪　You then move on to learning a dive cartwheel, in which you actually get some flight before putting your hands down.

✪　When you have succeeded in getting enough height before putting your hands down, you can go for the aerial move with the support of your coach and a thick mat.

✪　When you gain in confidence and skill you will be able to try the move unaided. For weeks you will continue to put your hands down at the last minute. Eventually you will perform the move on your own.

Sometimes when you manage to complete a move for the first time unaided, it fails to come off the second time you try it. Don't worry; if you manage it once you will certainly be

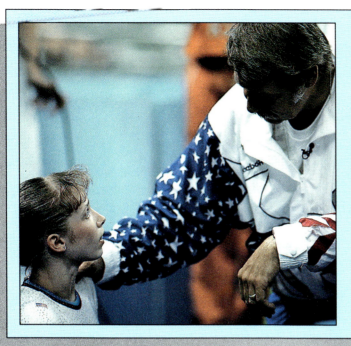

○ *Don't take criticism personally; your coach just wants you to improve your performance and achieve your potential.*
○ *If you don't understand something you are being told to do, ask your coach to talk you through it again.*
○ *If you feel uncomfortable with a movement, say so. Be honest with your coach.*
○ *Never go on to the apparatus unless there is a coach in the gym, even if it is to practise elements you think you know very well – this is dangerous.*

World champion Kim Zmeskal of the USA takes some advice and encouragement from coach Bela Karolyi.

able to manage it again, and in a short time the skill will become second nature and will work every time.

If you are learning something new, your coach will probably step in and support you through the movement. This is called spotting, and it allows you to go through the whole movement so that you know what it should feel like. When you have learned the individual parts of the move it will help you to bring them all together. Spotting should not be overdone though, because it can create a false feeling of confidence.

By using crash mats, a foam-filled pit or even a harness, you will also build up confidence once you begin to master a new skill. The main thing to remember is – don't push yourself too hard too soon. Learn the basics first before trying the complex elements. Don't get frustrated or angry if a new skill doesn't seem to be coming together as quickly as you would like. Persevere – you will get there in the end. Remember, it can take weeks, months or even years to learn a new move. If you are coming to the end of a training session but you can't quite master a new skill, leave it and try again tomorrow. Pushing yourself too hard when you are tired can lead to injury.

VAULT AND ASYMMETRIC BARS

The vault

The vault is the only piece of gymnastic apparatus on which you can gain or lose 10 marks in less than six seconds! It is a piece that many gymnasts love because it is so exhilarating. The horse itself is 120 cm high for women and 135 cm for men, but it can be lowered for junior gymnasts.

Women vault over a broad horse. There is no limit to the amount of steps they can take on the run-up, and they get two chances to perform either the same vault or two different ones. Men vault over a long horse and get just one chance to impress the judges. They are also limited on their run-up, which must not exceed 25 m.

A vault can be divided into three parts: the run-up and flight on to the

This gymnast demonstrates the energy and strength required for a successful vault.

Women vault over a broad horse and get two chances to impress the judges.

mind that if you have the board too close, your flight-on will be poor and this will lose you marks and reduce the forward movement of your flight-off.

You should spend a long time practising your run-up. Experiment by lengthening and shortening the run-up to see what works best, but remember to count the number of steps from your starting point to the springboard. This ensures that when you get to a competition you will be able to reproduce your run-up exactly.

Natalia Yurchenko had to measure her run-up to the last centimetre. The Soviet gymnast had a vault named after her when she was the first gymnast to run up and do a round-off (like a cartwheel, but the feet snap together in the air so that you land on two feet) on to the springboard before going backwards on to the horse into a Tsukahara.

Like all other gymnastic movements, vaulting is learned gradually. When you have perfected your run-up and rebound off the springboard, you will practise the vault with the help of your coach and plenty of crash mats. For example, when learning a handspring off the

horse (off a springboard); the vault itself; and flight-off and landing.

For each individual gymnast the run-up is different, and each gymnast has the springboard a preferred distance from the horse. There is no rule about this – you can have the board as far or as close as you like. The distance of the board from the horse changes depending on the vault you are doing. You need to bear in

box you will start with a very low box or box top, with mats piled up high, level with the other side of the apparatus. These can be gradually taken away as you gain in confidence and learn the skill.

The landing is an extremely important part of the vault. It is often the landing that decides the gold medal in top competition, and a bad landing can ruin a good vault. Practise your landing technique by jumping from different heights. You should stretch out in the air but on landing, bend through the knees and straighten out when you have gained your balance.

✪ Squat or through vault

You will start to learn this vault by running and jumping on to the springboard, placing the hands on the box and landing in a crouched position on top of it. You then jump off with an extended body position to land. When these two stages have been learned, the whole vault can be attempted. This involves the same technique but, instead of landing on the horse, place your hands on it. In a squatting position, point your legs straight out in front of you between your hands as you travel over the horse before

landing on the other side. Extend the legs out quickly after the squat position, and keep your head up throughout the vault. If you don't do these two things, your landing will turn into a nose-dive!

✪ Handspring

The run-up is the same as for a through vault, but you aim to fly on to the horse with your body higher than your hands. When you contact the apparatus you are propelled through the handstand position. Push off with your hands to produce a good flight-off before landing. In order to perform this vault well, you need a powerful run-up, strength and good body tension.

✪ Tsukahara

This vault, named after the Japanese gymnast Mitsuo Tsukahara, is only for advanced gymnasts, and it is the most common vault in top international competition. After the run-up, the gymnast does a half-turn on to the apparatus before the hands connect with the box. (When learning this vault you could practise the half-turn stage for a year or more before going any further.) After the push-off you need to get as much height and momentum as possible so as to

The Tsukahara
Concentrate on 'sticking' the landing (not moving the feet once they have landed). A poor landing will result in marks being deducted.

complete a full somersault before landing to face the horse.

The asymmetric bars

T he uneven, or asymmetric, bars are exclusive to the women's event. The high bar is 2.35 m from the ground, and the low bar is 1.55 m high. You can move the bars closer or further apart to suit yourself; however, these days most gymnasts prefer them as wide apart as possible, to make moves such as giant circles easier to perform. Recently the rails on the bars, which are made from fibreglass, have been made rounder and thinner. There is no time limit for a bars routine, but the exercise must include at least ten elements. In a good bars exercise you are aiming to show change of direction – swinging both forwards and backwards – and constant movement between the high and low bars. The routine should be flowing and smooth.

Of all the pieces in the women's event, the bars require the highest degree of body conditioning and strength, and for this reason they are the last piece that a gymnast learns. If you take up gymnastics it will probably be a couple of years before you learn anything of note on bars. So if you are already training and are bored of learning nothing more exciting than forward and backward swings, do not despair. It is necessary to build up strength by constant repetition of these exercises before moving to the more ambitious moves.

Kim Gwang Suk shows the confidence and polish that has made her one of the world's greatest performers on asymmetric bars.

Once you have built up enough strength to tackle this piece of apparatus, the possibilities are endless. The greatest performer on bars in the world today is Korea's Kim Gwang Suk. Although she is just 1.37 m tall, she is incredibly strong, and her spectacular bars routine won the gold medal in the 1991 World Championships.

✪ Lay-away back hip circle

From the front support position, swing the legs forwards, creating a pike position. From here you can get the momentum to swing the legs back and lift the whole body away from the bar. This is the lay-away. From this position you then swing the legs forwards again, and bring the hips back into the bar so that you can circle backwards over it, finishing in a front support. The key thing to remember when performing this element is to keep the body taut and the arms straight and strong.

✪ Giant swing

This is the most important element in modern competition and, if you hope to be a top gymnast, you will have to master this move early on. From a handstand on the top bar, it is basically a full 360-degree swing around the bar to handstand again, without touching the bottom bar. This move was introduced a few years ago in international competition by the Soviet gymnasts. It is a move taken directly from the men's high-bar routine, although it has been adapted slightly in that the body shape has to change in order to avoid hitting the lower bar. It is a move that requires a great deal of upper body strength and control.

Dismount
Keep the legs straight and strong in this movement.

✪ **Back-away**

This is a back somersault away from the top bar to land, and forms the basis for more complex dismounts that you may learn later. From a handstand you swing downwards, 'dishing' the body slightly to avoid the lower bar. Relax the hips and kick as you swing upwards again. As the bar is released (at about 45 degrees above horizontal), you somersault away from the bar to land.

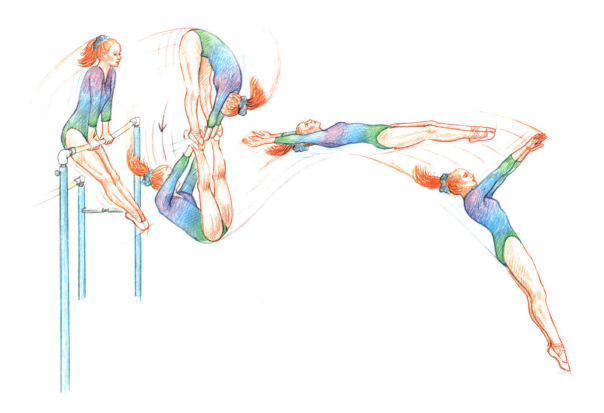

BEAM AND FLOOR

The beam

The beam is 10 cm in width, 5 m long, made of wood (slightly padded), and its height from the floor in top competition is 120 cm. The beam is generally the piece of apparatus that gymnasts fear the most, and it is regarded as the biggest challenge. The beam exercise lasts between 70 and 90 seconds, and includes acrobatics linked with dance steps and leaps, and must contain a 360-degree turn.

Beam skills have to be learned gradually. Elementary movements

China's Li Li makes the most of her strength and flexibility in this beam exercise.

are learned on the floor first, by practising on a line. You progress to a bench, which is obviously much wider than a beam and so helps to build up confidence. You then move on to a very low beam, gradually increasing the height of the beam as you become more sure of yourself.

When learning a new beam element you must immediately go back to learning the movement on the floor first, gradually going through the different height stages before performing the move on the full-height beam. Even the world's top gymnasts learn new moves in this way.

The beam is all about confidence and surety of movement. You should try to project as much confidence as possible during your routine. Try not to look down; if you are too nervous you will probably wobble or even come off the apparatus altogether. If this happens in competition it is not the end of the world. Simply take a deep breath, regain your composure and remount the apparatus to continue your exercise. Try not to let it affect your concentration.

Even the best beam exponents such as Nadia Comaneci, who scored the first ever 10 on beam in Montreal,

and Olga Korbut, who performed the first back somersault on beam, have fallen in competition at one time or another.

✪ Press to handstand

To start your exercise you need to mount the beam in an interesting way. One way of doing this is to stand on a springboard facing the beam. Place your hands on the beam and, rebounding off the springboard, press up to a handstand – straddling the legs sideways and up to the vertical. Hold the handstand before carrying on with the exercise, either by turning and walking out of the handstand or by coming down to side splits on the beam. This type of mount should be attempted only by a gymnast who has perfected her handstand technique on the floor first of all.

✪ Balance

Most gymnasts include a balance in their exercise. The arabesque is the most common. This involves standing on one leg and lifting the free leg behind to horizontal or beyond. The arms are stretched to the side with the standing leg perfectly straight and the free leg perfectly extended, right through to the toes.

**Handspring
dismount from
the beam**
Try not to flop off
the end of the
beam. Gain
height by pushing
off with the hands.

✪ Handspring dismount

You could dismount by handspringing off the end of the beam. This is the same as a handspring on the floor. From halfway along the beam you run and, placing your hands on the end of the beam, you push off into a handspring, landing with control on the other side. Having mastered this dismount you could then progress to learning an aerial dismount such as a straight front somi (somersault) off one leg, or a barani (a round-off with no hands).

The floor

When most people think about gymnastics it is probably the floor exercise that comes to mind first. It is performed on a 12 m square, which is extremely springy. The women perform their exercise to music and it lasts between 70 and 90 seconds. The men do not use music, and their exercise lasts between 50 and 70 seconds.

The women's floor exercise is choreographed around three tumbles

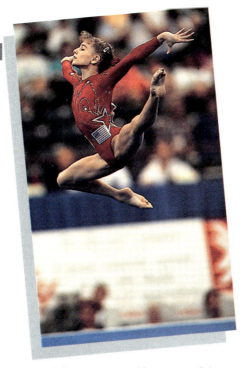

Shannon Miller, the USA's most successful gymnast at the Barcelona Olympics, shows tremendous elevation and extension in this side-jump.

Interpretation of music and expression of movement are essential in a floor routine. Henrietta Onodi of Hungary is one of the world's strongest performers on this piece of apparatus.

and, in top competition, one of these tumbles should include two somersaults. The routine should also contain different dance elements such as split jumps, pirouettes and balances as well as other gymnastic elements such as walkovers, handstands, etc. The music should be interpreted, so it is important that you choose music to suit your personality.

Apart from tumbling, men must show strength and control in their floor exercise. They must include a held balance and show changes of speed and direction.

This piece of apparatus gives you an ideal opportunity to show your

personality and style. Olga Korbut was famous for her cheeky choreography and even cheekier grin. Daniela Silivas' bright choreography and performance earned her the Olympic floor title in Seoul in 1988. Today's strongest floor workers include Kim Zmeskal and Svetlana Boguinskaia.

✪ Handstand with full turn

The handstand, the foundation of all gymnastic movements, can be included in a floor routine. It can be made into a more impressive element if you add a full turn. After holding the handstand position with full extension, move the hands around so that you

The flic

This is a travelling movement, so concentrate on achieving backward rather than upward momentum.

complete a 360-degree turn on your hands. Control the handstand at the end before bringing the legs down one at a time.

✪ **Round-off**

It would be impossible to have a floor routine without this move. It is like a cartwheel, but in the air the legs are snapped together so that you land on two feet. The round-off comes after a run-up and is often the first movement in tumbling sequences. It is used to turn the body backwards whilst moving forwards, and creates the power to launch you into a

tumbling run.

✪ **Flic or back-flip**

After a round-off you are in the perfect position of power to go into a back-flip. From two feet you jump backwards on to the hands, pushing off the hands to bring the legs over the top and down to the floor again. The main things to remember in a back-flip are:

✪ Keep the arms strong.

✪ If your arms collapse you will end up with a headache!

✪ It is backward momentum and not height that is important.

POMMEL HORSE AND RINGS

The pommel horse

The pommel horse is a vaulting horse with two wooden handles attached to the top. The horse stands 105 cm from the ground (it can be shortened to suit younger gymnasts) and the pommels are between 41 and 44 cm apart. There is no time limit for this exercise, although the routines usually last 30 seconds.

This is the exercise that causes the most problems for male gymnasts. It is the piece where even the world's best and most talented gymnasts have had disasters, with the exception perhaps of Zoltan Magyar of Hungary.

He dominated this piece of apparatus during the 1970s and early 1980s and was the greatest pommel worker of all time.

You need a lot of strength to perform a good pommel exercise, and the difficulty comes because the gymnast has to balance on one hand whilst swinging around the handles. The gymnast's legs circle around the horse during the exercise and can split to perform shears (the legs are straddled and pass over the end of the horse).

The legs and body must not touch the apparatus during the routine. If the exercise contains a handstand, as it usually does in top competition,

Pae Gil Suk demonstrates strength and control on the pommel – one of the most difficult pieces of apparatus.

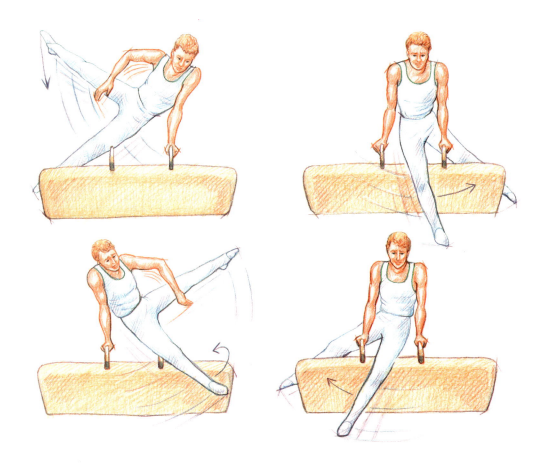

The shears
Try to keep the swinging movement as smooth as possible.

it must not be held. All three sections of the pommel horse must be used, which means that the gymnast must travel the length of the horse.

✪ **Double leg circle**

You learn this after you have mastered the single leg circle. You swing both legs round in front of the horse, lifting one hand as you go to enable the legs to pass to the front of the apparatus. As the legs pass to the front of the horse, you grip the pommels with both hands and then,

as the legs swing to the back again, the opposite hand is taken off. During the move the supporting arm and shoulder lean in towards the apparatus to counterbalance the movement of the legs. This movement is repeated several times at speed so that the legs are swinging round and round the apparatus but never touching it.

✪ **Shears**

This is a swing like a pendulum with the legs split very wide. The swing can be backwards or forwards but the legs cross over at the end of each swing. There is considerable transfer of weight as the gymnast swings from one side to the other.

❂ Flairs

This is basically a double leg circle but, instead of keeping the legs together, you split the legs wide in a windmill-type movement. It looks very spectacular and difficult but if you master the double leg circle it shouldn't be long before you can attempt this version of it.

The rings

To be a good rings performer you need strength, and lots of it. The rings are the most demanding of the men's exercises – mainly because of the extreme arm and shoulder strength required, together with absolute control and balance of movement, and good timing.

The top of the rings frame is 5.5 m from the floor, and the rings them-selves are suspended from the frame. The rings, which are made from wood and are attached to straps, which are in turn attached to wires, are 255 cm from the floor. Therefore it is

necessary for the coach to lift the gymnast on to the apparatus.

The rings exercise usually lasts between 40 and 60 seconds and must include swinging movements and three different strength moves. These must be held for at least two seconds. The most famous strength move is the crucifix. This involves the gymnast holding the rings with his arms out straight and his body hanging straight down with the toes pointed to the floor. The routine must also include two handstands, one from a swing and one from a strength move. During the exercise the gymnast must control the rings so

Solid as a rock! Vitaly Scherbo on his way to yet another Olympic gold medal for the CIS team in 1992.

that there is as little swing as possible. Top gymnasts prepare for dismount with a swing, and the dismount itself is usually a somersault.

✪ Half lever

With the arms locked straight and pushing down into the rings, the gymnast lifts the legs to a 90-degree angle. This lever position is held and demonstrates balance and strength. The main thing to remember is to keep the head up and the back absolutely straight.

✪ Handstand

From the half lever you can learn to lift to handstand. This requires a great deal of strength and control and of course must only be attempted if you have completely mastered the handstand on the floor first. The hips are lifted upwards with the legs until they are high enough to push up to the handstand position, which should be held and should involve as little swing of the rings as possible.

✪ Planche

Even advanced gymnasts find this move difficult. Keeping the shoulders well in front of the rings, the body is held horizontal and perfectly straight. Again, the rings must be as still as possible.

The lift to handstand
It is important to keep movement of the rings to a minimum.

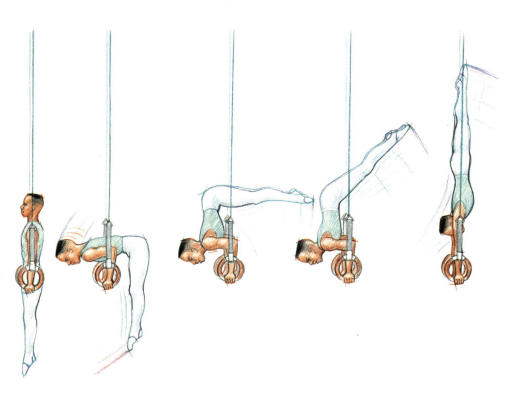

PARALLEL BARS AND HIGH BAR

◀ ◀ ◀ ◀

Great Britain's Neil Thomas shows his mastery of the parallel bars.

The parallel bars

A good parallel bars exercise should involve a combination of strength, suppleness, balance, flowing swings, releases and regrasps. The swinging movements occur above and below the bars, and any balances or handstands should be held, although the exercise must not include more than three stationary holds. The routine usually lasts around 20 seconds, although there is no time limit. There are penalties for touching the apparatus with the legs or body. The apparatus is for men only and consists of two wooden bars attached to a metal frame.

The bars stand 1.75 m above the floor but they can be adjusted for younger gymnasts. They are oval, 3.5 m long and are set from 42 to 48 cm apart. The wood used is quite springy, enabling the gymnast to gain

The straddle clip
The movement of the legs across the bars must be quick and sharp, so keep the legs very taut.

height when pushing off the bars for the release and regrasp moves and for the dismount. The world's top gymnasts, such as the world bars champion Li Jing, gain so much height for their dismount that they have enough time to complete an extremely difficult element, such as a double back somersault, before landing.

Young gymnasts learning the parallel bars for the first time have to 'break in' their upper arms before they progress on this apparatus. This is because to be able to perform an upper-arm support swing, the upper arm must remain in contact with the apparatus. This may hurt a bit at first but the upper arm muscles soon toughen up.

✪ **Long upstart**

This is one of the first moves that you learn. It starts with a swing under the bar with the feet close to the floor. You then bring your legs over your

Once you have learnt the basics, you can move on to the more complex elements, like this difficult swing by China's Li Jing.

head by pulling hard on the bar. The legs then shoot up and forwards so that the body ends up above the bars with the feet pointing straight down and the arms locked out straight.

✪ **Straddle clip**

This move requires quick leg movements and good co-ordination. Swing your body to the back of the bars, push hard and let go. Open your legs and straddle quickly over the top of the bars. Bring the legs together again and regrasp the bars behind you.

✪ **Support swing**

Swinging is 90 per cent of bars work. This swing must be smooth which means not moving the shoulders backwards and forwards too much on the swings. From a held handstand you 'dish' the body out of balance to swing the legs downwards between the bars. When the hips are above the line of the shoulders you press down against the bars to force the shoulders in front of the hands and extend the body. The movement is then reversed so that the legs swing back to handstand again. The arms should be straight at all times.

The high bar

W idely acclaimed as the most spectacular of the men's apparatus, this is the one everybody wants to win. The steel bar itself is 255 cm above the ground and is just over 2.5 cm thick. The exercise

contains mainly swinging circles (both giant circles and movements closer to the bar) and breathtaking release-and-catch movements, which are often named after the gymnast who invented them – for example, the Deltchev, the Gienger and the Tkachev.

The exercise, which lasts between 30 and 40 seconds, must be vigorous and continuous and must include twists and changes of grip. This is a

key point when first learning this piece of apparatus – knowing when to use a particular grip, such as palms facing forwards, or a reverse grip, in which the palms face the gymnast.

The dismount can be spectacular because of the speed that a gymnast can build up before releasing and flying away from the bar to land. The landing must be upright and controlled. The gymnast must not contact the uprights during the

The upstart
This forms the basis of many movements that you will learn on the bar.

Grigori Misutin gains tremendous height and shows great skill in this spectacular release-and-catch movement on the high bar.

of passing above the bar.

✪ Long swing

This is basically a smooth swing from handstand to handstand, with the gymnast moving 360 degrees around the bar. From an extended handstand position you dish the body slightly to produce the swing. The body is tense until you are about to pass under the bar. At this point you should relax the hips, producing a hollow shape. This helps the legs to speed up into the upswing. Once you pass under the bar there should be a slight angle between your shoulders and hips. This move will eventually form the basis of your high-bar routine. It can be used to build up to a dismount or to a spectacular release-and-catch move.

✪ Back away

As on the women's parallel bars, this is a back somersault away from the top bar to land, and forms the basis for more complex dismounts that you may learn later. From handstand you swing downwards as in the giant circle, open at the hips and kick as you swing upwards again and, as the bar is released (at about 45 degrees above horizontal), you somersault away from the bar to land.

exercise but he may be lifted on to the apparatus at the start of his routine by his coach.

✪ Upstart

This is one of the first moves that you learn. The legs are brought up to the bar from a slight swing. Pressing down very hard, you lift your body above the bar in the next swing to end in front support. This is the easiest way

COMPETITION DAY

You've been training all term, repeating exercises and routines until you are blue in the face, and then suddenly it arrives – the big day – the competition.

You've been working towards this for what seems like forever, so how come when you wake up your legs feel like jelly, you feel sick and you dread going out there to perform? Nerves are natural on competition days, and they can be very positive if you use them in the right way. However, if you are too nervous you will undoubtedly make mistakes.

Nerves are not the only reason why some gymnasts do not perform well in competition. Other factors, such as not being used to the apparatus and surroundings, or distractions in the competition hall, can affect performance. Competition is the best way to measure your progress, so turn it to your advantage and make the most of this opportunity to show off your skills and how much you have improved.

The traditional layout of a competition arena.

The CIS team are congratulated by the Romanians after winning team gold at the 1992 Barcelona Olympics.

Some useful tips

☻ *Don't train heavily the night before. Try to relax and get an early night.*

☻ *Organize your gym bag the evening before. Don't leave it until the last minute.*

☻ *Do not eat a heavy meal before competing. If possible, eat some carbohydrate, such as pasta or bread, a few hours before. This will give you energy. Don't fall into the trap of eating a lot of chocolate.*

☻ *If you begin to feel panic-stricken, take some deep breaths and tell yourself very firmly: 'It's just like any other day, I've practised these exercises a hundred times before, I've nothing to worry about.'*

☻ *When you arrive at the competition hall, get your bearings. Choose a feature like a pillar or window and relate it to something in your own gym. This will help you to work out where you will start and finish your floor exercise.*

☻ *Take into account where the judges will be sitting, and try to ensure that your best element – for example, a really extended balance or original acrobatic element – happens in front of the judges and not facing away from them.*

☻ *Concentrate during the warm-up as there may be several people warming up on the mat at once. Keep your wits about you and try not to get distracted.*

☻ *Before you go on, take a quiet moment to think through your exercise and imagine yourself performing the perfect routine.*

☻ *When your name is announced and you walk on, look confident even if you don't feel it.*

☻ *If you do make a mistake, take a deep breath and gather yourself together before carrying on.*

☻ *Most of all, enjoy the day. After all, competitions don't come round that often, and it is a great chance to prove yourself and show off your exercises. To win a medal is a brilliant feeling, but simply to perform your very best is just as satisfying.*

Judging a competition

There are four judges and a referee for each piece of apparatus. The judges are fairly close to the apparatus they are judging, so they can see faults in your exercise and deduct the relevant marks. Each judge writes down a score out of ten on a judging slip and hands it to the referee. The highest and lowest marks are disregarded, whilst the middle two marks are averaged to give the final score, which is shown on a scoreboard. However, in a world or European championship there are six judges on the panel. The highest and lowest marks are rejected, and it is the average of the middle four scores that gives the gymnast his or her final mark.

In artistic gymnastics the different elements or moves are graded according to difficulty, from A for the easiest moves through B and C to D for the hardest moves of all. World-class gymnasts like Kim Zmeskal of the USA include at least two B, three C and one D move in their exercises. An example of a C element would be a double tucked back-somersault.

Nelli Kim, Olympic floor champion in 1976, is now a top international judge.

For example, a fall from the apparatus will cost you 0.5 of a mark, but wobbles, bent arms or legs or lack of extension can cost you valuable tenths (0.1) of a mark each time the fault happens.

Top international competitions, such as the world or European championships, are divided into three parts. In the first competition all of the gymnasts perform compulsory exercises and then their voluntary routines. This part of the championship decides the team title. Each team has six gymnasts, but only the top five scores count towards the team total.

From this part of the competition the top thirty-six gymnasts, three per country, go forwards and perform their voluntary routines again. This decides the overall individual champion.

Then the finals on each piece of apparatus take place. The top eight gymnasts from the voluntary section of the first competition compete again for the individual apparatus titles. This gives those gymnasts who are very good on one piece (but perhaps not so strong on everything else) the chance to win a medal.

At international level, the splits is classed as a basic move in the floor exercise.

Of course not many gymnasts make it to world championship level, so most gymnasts should concentrate on A and B moves. When you are making up a floor exercise for competition your coach can tell you how many A and B moves you need to include. He or she will help you to produce a well-balanced exercise.

Your main concern should be to make as few mistakes in your routine as possible. All errors, no matter how small, will be penalized by the judges.

RHYTHMIC GYMNASTICS

This exciting, colourful and innovative branch of the sport made its Olympic debut in Los Angeles in 1984. It was developed into the sport that exists today by the Eastern Europeans in the 1950s and 1960s. So well-developed is the sport in countries such as Bulgaria, that a top rhythmic gymnast such as Bianka Panova is as famous in her country as a football star such as Paul Gascoigne is in Britain.

Since the first rhythmic gymnastics championships in 1963, the sport has been dominated by the USSR – now teams from the former Soviet Union – and Bulgaria. Recent years have seen the emergence of the Koreans and Spanish as medal contenders.

The first rhythmic gymnast ever to score 10 in an international event was Bianka Panova of Bulgaria, who is considered to be one of the greatest competitors in rhythmic gymnastics. Today the stars include Bulgaria's Maria Petrova, and Alexandra Timochenko and Oksana Skaldina, who are both from the same club in Kiev in the Ukraine.

The gymnasts use five pieces of hand apparatus: rope, hoop, ball, clubs and ribbon. They perform on a 12 m square, and each exercise is performed to music. The routines last between 60 and 90 seconds and are made up of body movements such as bends, balances, turns, leaps and dance steps. During the routine the apparatus is kept moving all the time with throws, swings and circles, etc.

As well as the individual event

Perfection of movement – Timochenko extends to the maximum in this back flexion.

Alexandra Timochenko shows the grace, flexibility, strength and balance that have taken her to the top in rhythmic gymnastics.

there is a group competition. This involves a team of six gymnasts performing an exercise at the same time. This is spectacular to watch because of frequent exchanges of apparatus and intricate floor patterns and choreography. Often the six pieces of apparatus are not all the same; for example, three gymnasts might have hoops whilst the other three have ropes or balls.

There is a great emphasis on dance in rhythmic gymnastics, and many of the movements are taken from ballet. Because of this, the qualities needed to be a top rhythmic gymnast are different from those needed by artistic gymnasts. For example, you need to be exceptionally supple, have good leg strength and control, good dance ability, quick reactions, stamina and imagination. Throws with the apparatus can go as high as 10 m into the air, so the gymnast needs good throwing technique as well as strength.

The judges look out for good lines in balances and turns, so the gymnasts are usually quite tall and slim – in fact they look very much like ballet dancers. Each exercise is marked out of ten, with points being deducted for dropping the apparatus, poor execution, stepping outside the area, time faults and, occasionally, inappropriate dress!

✪ **Rope:** The rope is made of hemp or synthetic material and is cut to suit the height of the gymnast. It has no handles, although most gymnasts knot the ends to make the rope easier to catch. Besides skipping and throws, the gymnasts perform complex lasso-type movements and releases-and-catches with the rope.

✪ **Hoop:** The hoop can be made of wood or plastic (although most gymnasts choose plastic because it is more practical), and is 90-100 cm in diameter. Besides being thrown the hoop can be rotated on the hand or other parts of the body, rolled on the floor (or body), and leapt over and through.

✪ **Ball:** The ball is made of plastic and must be between 57 and 62 cm in circumference. The minimum weight is 400 g, and it is thrown, rolled, swung, spun and bounced.

✪ **Clubs:** The clubs are made of plastic or wood, are 40-50 cm in length and weigh a minimum of 150 g each. The clubs are circled, rotated, thrown, juggled and rolled. They are often considered the most difficult piece and are usually the last piece a gymnast learns. You will probably develop sore hands when first learning to throw and catch this piece of apparatus, but the hands toughen up quickly.

✪ **Ribbon:** The ribbon is made of silk, 4-6 cm wide and 6 m in length. The first metre is double thickness. The minimum weight of the ribbon is 35 g. The stick is made of fibreglass, 50-60 cm in length, and must be less than 1 cm in diameter. It has an attachment on the end, usually a swivel and hook, that joins the stick to the ribbon. Often described as the most spectacular of the apparatus, the ribbon is circled, spiralled, snaked and thrown and, like all the other pieces, must be kept moving all the time.

Keeping fit at home

Time in the gym is precious, so you can give yourself a head start and do a lot of groundwork at home. There are plenty of simple exercises that you can do to increase your flexibility and improve stamina, and they don't require a lot of space.

✪ *Use time watching television to flex and point the feet alternately and stretch out the toes. This improves ankle flexibility – fairly important when you consider how much gymnasts use their feet.*

✪ *Do press-ups to improve arm strength.*

✪ *Do sit-ups for toning stomach muscles.*

✪ *Stand with your feet on the edge of a step, hold a wall or banister for support, and gently rise on to the balls of the feet and lower. Repeat this twenty times. This stretches out and strengthens calf muscles.*

✪ *Raising the leg as high in front of you as possible and keeping your supporting leg straight, hold the raised leg straight and taut for ten seconds. This can be repeated to the side and back, and improves leg strength and balance.*

✪ *An old inner tube from a bicycle tyre hooked around the leg of your bed is very effective for building up leg strength. By hooking your foot inside the tube and constantly extending and pushing the leg away from it, you build up the inner thigh muscles. This piece of apparatus can also be used to build up arm strength.*

LIFE AFTER COMPETITION

Gymnastics produces some of the youngest champions of any sport. At fourteen, Nadia Comaneci became the youngest Olympic champion ever in Montreal.

Because gymnasts tend to be slight, people think that once you hit fifteen you are past your peak. That is not true – top gymnast Svetlana Boguinskaia is nineteen and still

It's good to win but it's just as important to be a gracious loser.

wins world titles. Rhythmic gymnasts don't really reach their full potential until at least nineteen, and can go on competing until much later.

So what if you decide that your training days are over but you still want to be involved in the sport? Well, there are plenty of options. Many gymnasts go on to become coaches. In the world's leading gymnastics nations, it is taken for granted that once you have finished competing you go on to train others. In the republics of the former Soviet Union there are special sports schools, where top athletes can train intensively on a daily basis. In these institutes there is a very high ratio of coaches to gymnasts, which means that one coach trains just a handful of pupils. Therefore, there is always a demand for coaches, who are paid a wage just as in any other job. In Britain very few coaches are paid, and most of them give up their spare time freely because they love the sport.

Former champions such as Nelli Kim and Olga Korbut turned to coaching after their retirement from the sport. Nadia Comaneci, who now coaches in the USA, also makes television appearances and performs in demonstration events.

In fact you don't have to retire to become a coach. It is possible to get coaching qualifications whilst still competing yourself, and many clubs encourage their gymnasts to coach each other and choreograph exercises for the younger gymnasts.

Many former gymnasts go on to become judges. This requires a great knowledge of the sport and of the Code of Points. You need to pass several exams before you can become a judge, but judging is a discipline that provides an exciting challenge for many who have competed themselves.

So when the time comes for you to hang up your gym shoes, there are still ways to be involved and contribute to the development of the sport. And remember, gymnastics teaches many qualities that are invaluable for other parts of your life. Discipline, courage, determination and a competitive edge are characteristics that are useful at school, at college and at work. Someone once said that becoming a gymnast was the best career move I ever made – and I really couldn't argue with that!

INTERNATIONAL COMPETITIONS

Gina Gogean of Romania on the beam during the 1992 Olympic Games.

Olympic Games: held every four years.
 1992 overall champions: Men - Vitaly Scherbo (CIS)
                                    Women - Tatiana Gutsu (CIS)

World championships: these are held every year. However, there are two types of world championship, which alternate. The first competition includes the team competition and the individual all-round championship. The following year there is an apparatus world championship, which decides the world champions on each piece. Every four years a big meeting is held involving all competitions.
1991 overall champions: Men - Grigori Misutin (CIS)
                                   Women - Kim Zmeskal (USA)

European championships: held every two years.
1992 overall champions: Men - Igor Korobchinski (Ukraine)
                                   Women - Tatiana Gutsu (Ukraine)

Commonwealth Games: held every four years.
1990 overall champions: Men - Curtis Hibbert (Canada)
                                   Women - Lori Strong (Canada)

Glossary

Arabesque   A balance on one leg with the free leg extended behind.

Barani   A round-off with no hands.

Carbohydrate   Starchy food, such as bread, potatoes and pasta, which gives energy.

Choreography   Dance steps and movements linked together and included in gymnastic exercises.

Crash mats   Thick foam-filled mats used when learning new skills.

Dishing   A slight curving of the body that happens usually in swinging movements on the bars.

Fibreglass   Springy, synthetic material used to make the high bar and asymmetric bars.

First position   A ballet position of the feet in which the legs and heels are together and the feet turn out as far as possible.

Flight-off   The height and momentum gained after you push off the horse before landing.

Flex   The opposite of to point.

Free cartwheel   A cartwheel with no hands.

Gienger   A somersault move on the high bar and asymmetric bars.

Momentum   The force of a moving body.

Pike   A body position in which the legs are at right angles to the body.

Pirouette   A turn on one foot.

Split jumps   A jump from one foot in which the gymnast forms the splits position in the air before landing on the front foot.

Spotting   When the coach helps a gymnast through a new movement.

Tkachev   A release move in which the gymnast's legs straddle over the top bar/high bar before he or she recatches the bar.

Tsukahara   A vault involving a somersault after the gymnast pushes off the box.

Tumbling   A series of acrobatic elements joined together in a sequence.

Further information

Useful addresses

Australian Gymnastics
Federation
2-6 Redwood Drive
Dingley
Victoria 3172
Australia

British Amateur Gymnastics
Association (BAGA)
Ford Hall
Lilleshall
National Sports Centre
Shropshire TF10 9NB
England

Canadian Gymnastics
Federation
Suite 510
1600 James Naismith
Avenue
Gloucester
Ontario K1B 5N4
Canada

Fédération Internationale de
Gymnastique (FIG)
Rue des Oeuches 10
2740 Moutier 1
Switzerland

New Zealand Gymnastics
Federation
23 Livingstone Street
PO Box 21116
Christchurch
New Zealand

United States Gymnastic
Federation
Pan American Plaza
Suite 300
201 F. Capitol
Indianapolis IN46225
USA

Further reading

The Complete Book Of Gymnastics by David Hunn (Ward Lock, 1978)

Gymnastic Skills by Norman Barrett and David Jefferis (Wayland, 1993)

Men's Gymnastics Coaching Manual by Lloyd Readhead (Springfield Books Ltd, 1987)

Modern Rhythmic Gymnastics by Jenny Bott (EP Sport, 1981)

The Puffin Book Of Gymnastics by Peter Ackroyd (Puffin, 1988)

The Superbook Of Gymnastics by Brian Hayhurst (Kingfisher Books, 1986)

Women's Gymnastics by Jill Coulton (EP Publishing, 1989)

Index

Numbers in **bold** refer to captions.